SING MUSICAL THEATRE

INTERMEDIATE (GRADES 4–5)

OVER THE RAINBOW

AND 14 OTHER SONGS FROM THE SHOWS

Selected and edited by John Gardyne and Luise Horrocks

TRINITY
COLLEGE LONDON

FABER *ff* MUSIC

© 2011 by Faber Music Ltd and Trinity College London
First published in 2011 by Faber Music Ltd in association with Trinity College London
Bloomsbury House
74–77 Great Russell Street
London WC1B 3DA
Music processed by SEL Engraving
Cover design by Lydia Merrills-Ashcroft
Printed in England by Caligraving Ltd
All rights reserved

CD produced and arranged by Paul Honey
© 2011 by Faber Music Ltd and Trinity College London
℗ 2011 by Faber Music Ltd and Trinity College London

ISBN10: 0-571-53557-7
EAN13: 978-0-571-53557-6

To buy Faber Music or Trinity publications or to find out about the full range of titles available,
please contact your local music retailer or Faber Music sales enquiries:

Faber Music Ltd, Burnt Mill, Elizabeth Way, Harlow, CM20 2HX England
Tel: +44(0)1279 82 89 89   Fax: +44(0)1279 82 89 90
sales@fabermusic.com   fabermusicstore.com

INTRODUCTION

This book contains 15 songs from a wide variety of shows and movies – some very well known, others less so – which offer a range of performing challenges suitable for intermediate-level singing and musical theatre students.

The best musical theatre songs are self-contained playlets in which a character – or a group of characters – in a specific dramatic setting explores an idea, learns something, makes a decision or changes in some way. It is the performer's job to convey this process to the audience with clarity, conviction and understanding.

In order to do this it is essential that the performer knows where the character is, what is happening in the story at that point, who the character is singing to and why s/he is expressing these ideas at that moment. So in the **BACKGROUND** to each song we have provided some key information about plot, characters and the dramatic situation, along with a brief summary of the production history of the musical from which it comes. But these are only the bare bones. There is no substitute for careful, detailed research and we would encourage performers to listen to recordings, attend performances, read librettos and find out as much as they can about these – and other – musicals and the writers and theatre professionals who created them. All this information will feed into your performance and make it richer, more detailed and more rewarding for both you and your audience.

The **PERFORMANCE NOTES** offer some starting points for interpretation and performance. These are intended to offer suggestions and are in no way intended to represent a 'definitive' rehearsal technique. Many of the observations and acting approaches can be applied to other songs in the collection (and indeed elsewhere), so we hope that as students and their teachers explore the different songs in the book they will develop a variety of approaches to preparation and rehearsal which they can apply to a range of repertoire.

In some cases, performers who are singing individual numbers from a show – where the original context may be impossible to recreate or would be too confusing for an audience – may choose to experiment with new approaches and make some innovative performance choices. A solo number might be shared between two or more performers, a duet sung as a solo, a song by a female character be sung by a man or vice versa, or the song re-imagined in a completely different dramatic situation, providing new perspectives and illuminating new meanings in the lyrics. The world of musical theatre has a rich tradition of this process (sometimes referred to as *de-contextualisation*) and we have included some suggestions on this that you might consider. But be careful. However you may re-invent a number – and the possibilities for doing so may be immense – always make sure that all the lyrics make sense and that the song as a whole retains an essential integrity and coherence.

The **SINGING TIPS** provide some technical exercises appropriate to the particular style or demands of each number. We are not suggesting that individual exercises should be used solely in the preparation of that one song and these may prove useful in working on others. Our intention is that over time students will build up a range of techniques which will help them develop their singing along with their acting and movement skills.

The CD contains backing tracks for each of the 15 songs. While these may be used in performance, they are intended primarily as an aid to rehearsal and preparation. Again, tempi and dynamics provide a starting point only and are not intended to be 'definitive'. Performers who have the opportunity to work with a piano accompanist should explore the musical possibilities of each score, which will enable them to further refine and nuance their performances and to make them uniquely personal, uniquely their own.

John Gardyne
Chief Examiner in Drama and Speech Subjects, Trinity College London

Luise Horrocks,
Singing teacher and Associate Chief Examiner, Trinity College London

BEAUTIFUL

MORT

BACKGROUND

Terry Pratchett is one of the most prolific and successful novelists in the world, with global sales of over 65 million books in 37 languages. The first of his comic fantasy Discworld novels was published in 1983 and this musical adaptation of *Mort* – the fourth book in the series – was produced by Youth Music Theatre UK[†] in 2007.

Librettist Jenifer Toksvig writes about this song: 'Mort grew up on the farm, just him and his Dad, and he's never really had much to do with girls. Then he gets a job as Death's apprentice, and falls in love at first sight with Princess Keli (as you do). Being a very logical sort of fifteen-year-old, this is a very Mort sort of song.'

PERFORMANCE NOTES

It's important that you don't play Mort as a caricature 'geek' or send him up in any way. Of course he's inarticulate and unsophisticated and lives in a parallel universe to our own, but that doesn't mean his emotions are any less heartfelt or his pain and anguish are any less real than anyone else's.

Mort is experimenting with language and melody. He longs to sing the most beautiful, eloquent love song in the world, but no sooner has he begun than he starts qualifying and modifying what he has said, his thoughts spinning off in all directions.

The composer's comments on the score are particularly helpful for the performer, showing how changes of tempo and delivery reflect Mort's thought processes. Mark the stages of his journey with care, precision and honesty. Then don't be afraid to really sing out 'with wild abandon' as you repeat Keli's name over and over again. It's a wonderful moment of clarity and release. But, Mort being Mort, he has to worry about things just one more time before the song ends.

SINGING TIPS

There are some short phrases in this song which help to suggest someone working things out as they go along. Try speaking the words out loud in time to get a feel for the complex rhythms and the ebb and flow of the thoughts. Clap the pulse of the music as you speak but be prepared to change the underlying tempo a little to suggest the unfolding moods.

Let your voice open up as you repeat the name *Ke-li*. The *k* sound is called a *plosive* consonant. Exaggerate the *k* and feel the force of the air. The *l* sound lifts the tongue up to ridge of the gum. If you exaggerate this you will feel how it almost stops the sound. When you're singing use the *k* to give you a strong start but then flip the tongue out of the way quickly so as to let the vowel on *i* carry the sound. Try holding your hands by the side of your head as you sing the quavers on *ke*, and then throw them forward on the *li*. Keep your hands forward as you sustain the *i* and feel the sound travelling forward from the ends of your fingers.

[†] Youth Music Theatre UK was founded in 2003 and is now Britain's largest organisation providing participation in musical theatre projects and productions for young people. For more information about Youth Music Theatre UK, its Musical Theatre Library and how to perform this work, go to www.youthmusictheatreuk.org.

BEAUTIFUL

LYRICS BY JENIFER TOKSVIG
MUSIC BY DOMINIC HASLAM

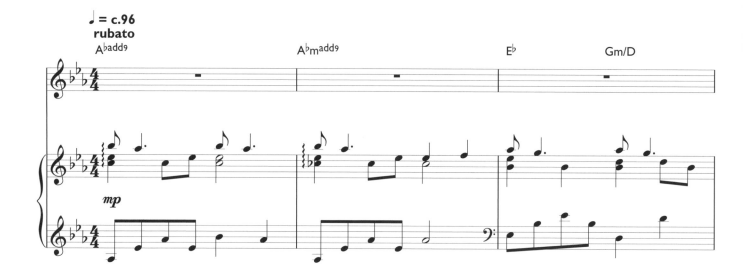

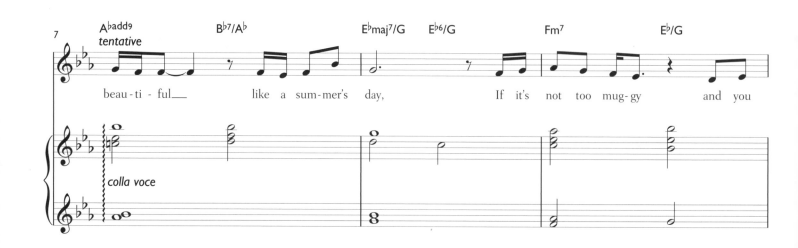

10

FEED THE BIRDS

MARY POPPINS

BACKGROUND

Walt Disney's 1964 film *Mary Poppins* received 13 Oscar nominations and won five, including Julie Andrews for Best Actress in her first screen role. A stage version, rewritten and with some new songs, opened in London in 2004.

London 1910: Mr and Mrs Banks can't control their wayward children Jane and Michael. One day the mysterious Mary Poppins flies into their lives. She becomes the children's governess, takes them on a series of magical adventures, and ends up reuniting the troubled family. After another busy day she sings this lullaby to the children at bedtime.

PERFORMANCE NOTES

At first glance, this looks like a very straightforward song – a simple, sentimental lullaby to send the children off to sleep. But even though the tempo is marked 'slowly, with feeling', it's essential that you don't allow yourself to become too languid and dreamy. Focus intensely on engaging your audience with the story you have to tell, right from the beginning of the song.

When you look at the lyrics more carefully, all kinds of questions arise. Who exactly is this strange old woman? What brings her to the steps of St Paul's Cathedral every day? Where are her family and friends? Individually or as a group you might work to give her an imagined life story. Then consider what relationship she might have with you – the person singing the song. A friend? A parent? A long-lost relative? Experiment with different choices and see how this changes your performance.

In the second verse the lyrics become even more mysterious and spiritual. Where exactly are the 'saints and apostles'? Is she referring to the cathedral statues or are they somehow actually *there*? And who is this 'you' who knows they are smiling even though they can't be seen? How does the refrain 'Feed the birds, tuppence a bag' gain in resonance and meaning as the song progresses? And what message does it leave with the audience?

In the stage adaptation, 'Feed the birds' is sung as a duet between Mary Poppins and the Bird woman. You might like to try this out. How do you think this might alter the audience's response?

SINGING TIPS

Smooth lines with even breath pressure sustaining a resonant sound are key to this song, with its long legato phrases. Ensure that your ribcage doesn't collapse as you exhale. Remember not to get lazy in your delivery: feel the phrases travelling forwards with musical purpose. Try the following to help feel the air flow and to improve stamina:

Imagine that your fingers are candles. There's a flame at the tip of each finger. Hold your fingers in front of your mouth and blow out the flames one by one, feeling the quick burst of air needed. Now take just one imaginary flame and blow it very gently. Don't allow it to be extinguished but keep sufficient air moving so that the flame bends. Now do the same, still holding the finger in front of your mouth, gently singing an *oo*. Sustain this for as long as you can but don't strain or let the quality of the sound deteriorate. Are you still making sure your ribcage hasn't collapsed?

FEED THE BIRDS

TRACK 2

WORDS AND MUSIC BY RICHARD M SHERMAN AND ROBERT B SHERMAN

I CAN HEAR THE BELLS

HAIRSPRAY

BACKGROUND

Based on the 1988 film by cult director John Waters, *Hairspray* is set in the racially segregated world of Baltimore in the early 1960s. Like *Grease* before it, the show centres around a local high school with a cast of larger-than-life characters and a score that parodies the popular musical styles of the time. *Hairspray* was a hit when it opened on Broadway in 2002. Many other productions have followed all over the world, and a film version was released in 2007.

'Pleasantly plump' teenager Tracey Turnblad dreams of appearing on the *Corney Collins Dance Show* on local television. When auditions for the show are announced, Tracey jumps at the chance and (literally) bumps into teen heart-throb Link Larkin at the studio. Thrilled and overcome, she immediately starts planning their future together.

PERFORMANCE NOTES

Although this is clearly a comic song – an absurd flight of fancy based on a tiny chance encounter with Link – it's important that you fully engage with Tracey's hopes and dreams in performance. This really is a life-changing moment for her.

The song starts with a moment of wonder and magic. Can you really believe this has actually happened? Use the strong rhythm and syncopated beat from bar 10 onwards to underpin your growing sense of self-belief. You know you're not a supermodel, but that's not the point – 'a girl who looks like me' is just as entitled to love as anyone else.

In the middle section ('Round 1 ...') your fantasies develop with perfect logic but at a dizzying speed as you move from first date to marriage in a few bars. In the show the number becomes a full-on, elaborately staged fantasy sequence. In rehearsing for a solo performance you might experiment with ways of conveying your dreams and enacting some of these events with just a few props. Don't let this get too complex or over-fussy though – keep the relentless forward movement of the song going, powered by your happiness and unshakeable belief that this will all come to pass.

SINGING TIPS

A full, warm sound is required in this song. Remember not to push your voice (using too much air to produce the sound) as this will result in a forced tone. Instead, think of the sound travelling forward.

Start by humming on one note. Try to feel the vibration on your lips or at the front of your mouth. Next, start on a hum and then move into an *oo*. Now try the following:

Hold your hands up by your head with your palms facing the ceiling. Sing an *ee*. As you're singing, move your hands slowly up and then forward. Feel the sound travelling away from you with your hands. Now do the same but this time change to an *ar* sound as your hands reach their highest point. Keep singing *ar* as you move your hands forward. As you're doing all this, make sure your lower body remains firm and grounded, with knees nice and loose and weight evenly balanced between the feet. If you can, practise these exercises looking out of a window to a far point. If you don't have a view from your window, imagine the sound travelling across a park to a distant horizon.

I CAN HEAR THE BELLS

MUSIC BY MARC SHAIMAN
LYRICS BY MARC SHAIMAN AND SCOTT WITTMAN

TRACK
3

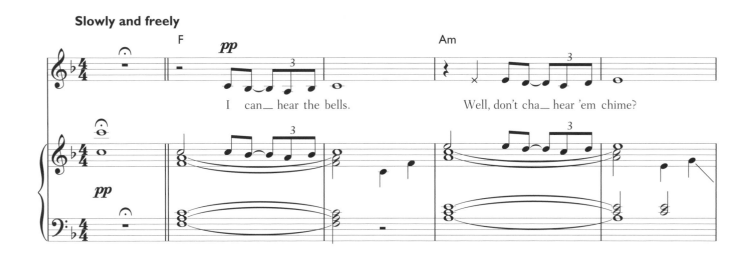

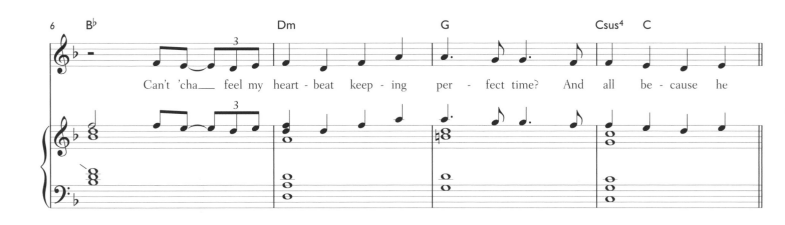

I LOVE PARIS

CAN-CAN

BACKGROUND

The songs of Cole Porter (1891–1964) have an elegant, witty, bittersweet quality that perfectly epitomises the popular ideal of sophisticated Manhattan high society in the 1930s and 1940s. *Can-Can* opened in New York in 1953 and ran for 829 performances, subsequently being made into a rather lacklustre film.

When the provocative can-can dance is banned by the authorities in 1890s Paris, night club owner La Môme Pistache and her dancing girls are thrown in jail. But the court judge falls in love with her and all ends happily. In this song the triumphant Pistache celebrates the unique appeal of her city.

PERFORMANCE NOTES

At first glance this simple, rather repetitive lyric may not seem to offer much for the performer. After a brief introduction the singer tells us she (or he) loves Paris at various times of year. In the second verse this idea is repeated word for word. The challenge is to make these ideas fresh, new and exciting and to create and sustain a sense of profound personal engagement right until the end.

The clue is in the final line, when you sing about your 'love'. Work backwards from this point. Create a history of your love affair, with memorable incidents at different times of the year – a bit like a montage of scenes from a film. Aim to make these as vivid as possible. If you went for a walk along the banks of the Seine, decide what the weather was like, what time of day it was, what were you wearing, what sounds, smells and tastes you remember. Enjoy re-living those perfect days.

As you sing, share these precious memories from the past as they jump into your head. Let them lead you to the realisation that the person with whom you shared those days really is 'my love'. Then, use the reprise to celebrate the future: every springtime, every fall, every rain shower, every corner of the city will have its own wonderful magic now you are together. If the first verse is in black-and-white, the second is in 3-D technicolour. No wonder you love Paris.

SINGING TIPS

With the repetition in this song you need to work on changing the tone colours of your voice so that your singing stays interesting and engaging. One way to experiment with the different sounds your voice can produce is to practise 'emotional scales'.

Sing a descending scale in a comfortable range to a vowel sound of your choice. Now sing the same scale angrily. What did you do to convey this feeling, and what happened to the sound? Try doing the same with different emotions: a happy scale, a sad scale, a timid scale or a proud scale. Listen to the sound and feel what you're doing differently to achieve these emotions. You might like to look in the mirror to see how your face changes as you sing. Just make sure you're not forcing or pushing, and always maintain good posture.

When you come to sing the song, think how the different colours you have practised can highlight the different pictures that are painted. Does the music help by using both a major and a minor key?

I LOVE PARIS

WORDS AND MUSIC BY COLE PORTER

TRACK 4

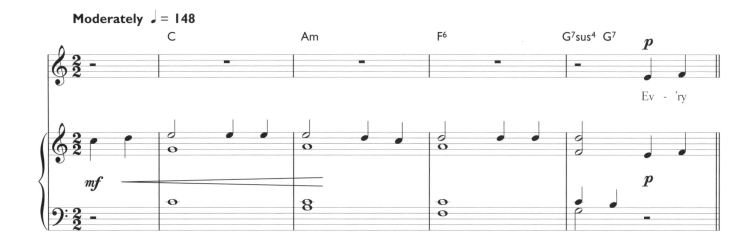

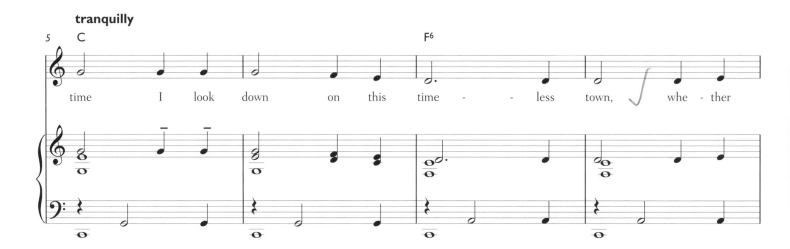

I WANT TO GO HOME

BIG

BACKGROUND

The comedy-fantasy movie *Big*, starring Tom Hanks – one of the most successful and popular films of the 1980s – provided the inspiration for the musical stage adaptation, which opened on Broadway in 1996.

12-year-old Josh Baskin longs to be grown up. A mysterious arcade game called 'Zoltar Speaks' grants him his wish and the next morning he finds himself in the body of a 30-year-old man. Thinking he is an intruder, his mother drives him out of his home. Josh makes his way to New York and spends the night, friendless and alone, at the Port Authority Bus Terminal.

PERFORMANCE NOTES

From the outset it's essential that the audience realise you're in an environment that is entirely new to you and which you find both exciting and threatening. How might you enter the stage and physicalise your performance to make this clear? You might consider using a few simple props, costumes or pieces of furniture to help you. If you're working with a group, creating the world of the late-night bus terminal might provide a starting point for some interesting improvisation exercises.

Your initial excitement at having 'an adventure' disappears in just a few seconds as 'this guy' takes out a knife. But a few moments later you're comforted by the 'friendly' people – until you see the bearded girl, that is. Don't be afraid to make these contrasts clear and sudden: these rapidly shifting, sometimes contradictory observations and responses combine to create a sense of this artless 12-year-old observing the world and will help you produce a richly comic performance. There's certainly no need to adopt an exaggerated childlike voice.

Note how Josh makes reference to TV shows (*Star Trek*) and technology ('3-D CD ROM') and uses wordplay ('the fickle finger flicked and it picked me'). Why do you think he does this? The ideas appear out of nowhere and disappear just as quickly. What does this tell you about his state of mind? This contrasts sharply with the more simple and heartfelt language of childhood ('Can I go now?' 'I want to go home') which gradually predominates as the song progresses. Use the repeated phrases of the final section to bring the song to a conclusion. The simple desire to be away from this dark, strange place, to be back home safely with your mother, is one which audiences of all ages will understand.

SINGING TIPS

Notice all the changes of tempo in this song as you move between elation and anxiety. Keep the excited sections moving forward (though without rushing) and then be prepared to slow down as you realise how alone and scared you feel. Rather like a comedian telling a joke, make sure the 'punchlines' are very clearly delivered.

Think of tonal contrasts too. Try experimenting with different gestures: where you feel adventurous, try opening your arms out, imagining that you're occupying a huge space. As you lose confidence, draw your hands in and feel your body getting smaller. Try walking around as you sing boldly and then standing still for the more frightened singing. How do the dynamics change as you do this?

I WANT TO GO HOME

WORDS AND MUSIC BY RICHARD MALTBY AND DAVID SHIRE

Moderately ♩ = 110

mp poco cresc. Con pedale

mp This is ex-cit-ing. It's an ad-ven-ture. I get to

sempre legato

see some things that most kids nev-er do. *poco rubato* That guy just took a knife out of his

LEGALLY BLONDE

LEGALLY BLONDE

BACKGROUND

Legally Blonde began life as a novel by Amanda Brown, inspired by her experiences at Stanford Law School in the 1990s. The 2001 movie starring Reese Witherspoon as Elle Woods was a huge popular hit and the musical stage adaptation opened in New York in 2007 and in London in 2009.

When fashion-mad Californian party girl Elle is dumped by her boyfriend, she follows him to Harvard Law School to win him back. The snobby law students see her as an airheaded bimbo, but she gradually earns their respect and gets an internship with courtroom shark Professor Callaghan. When Elle rejects Callaghan's advances he sacks her. With her legal career in ruins, she realises she has no choice but to 'leave with what's left of [her] dignity' and return to her parents in California.

PERFORMANCE NOTES

When performing this song, it's important to clearly visualise the future you envisage for yourself (driving along in a convertible, lying on a sunny beach, laughing with old friends and so on) and to make these images clear and vivid for the audience. While to most people this lifestyle might seem highly desirable, for you it represents total defeat. You have come a long way over the course of the show, and have become a much more sophisticated and mature person. Returning to a superficial life in your 'very small pond' represents the end of your dreams.

Elle's only real friend is scruffy assistant law teacher Emmett Forrest, who has helped her since she arrived. In this scene Emmett enters at around bar 70 and Elle thanks him for his support and says goodbye. You tentatively suggest that you might keep in touch: what does that suggest about your feelings for Emmett and how will this affect the delivery of the lyrics? If you're performing the song as a solo you still need to make it very clear that you're talking to – or at least about – a specific person at this point. Explore ways of creating a sense of this person – maybe by using a photo, a letter, some personal possession or gift.

Use your mounting anger to fuel the final verse, in which you can give full vent to your frustration and disappointment. 'Some girls' struggle and achieve great things but some are 'just meant to smile'. Is that really all you amount to? The song ends with your self-esteem in tatters, your one friend gone and a plea to 'just let me be'. Experiment with how – and how much – you might struggle to maintain a shred of dignity in these final moments.

SINGING TIPS

The emotion of this song builds from the quiet sadness of the opening through the passionate outpouring of the middle section and then back to a reflective finish. To help make this work, think of a gradual building of layers of sound and aim for a variety of tonal colours.

At the beginning and end, sing quietly and relatively freely, fitting the words round the chords in an almost conversational way. Try adding a hint of sobbing into the singing. As you move through the song you could add moments of breathiness too, helping to portray the emotion. Make sure your tone never becomes too nasal with all the *n* sounds in words such as 'pond', 'fine', 'blonde', 'sun' and 'known'.

LEGALLY BLONDE

MUSIC AND LYRICS BY LAURENCE O'KEEFE AND NELL BENJAMIN

TRACK 6

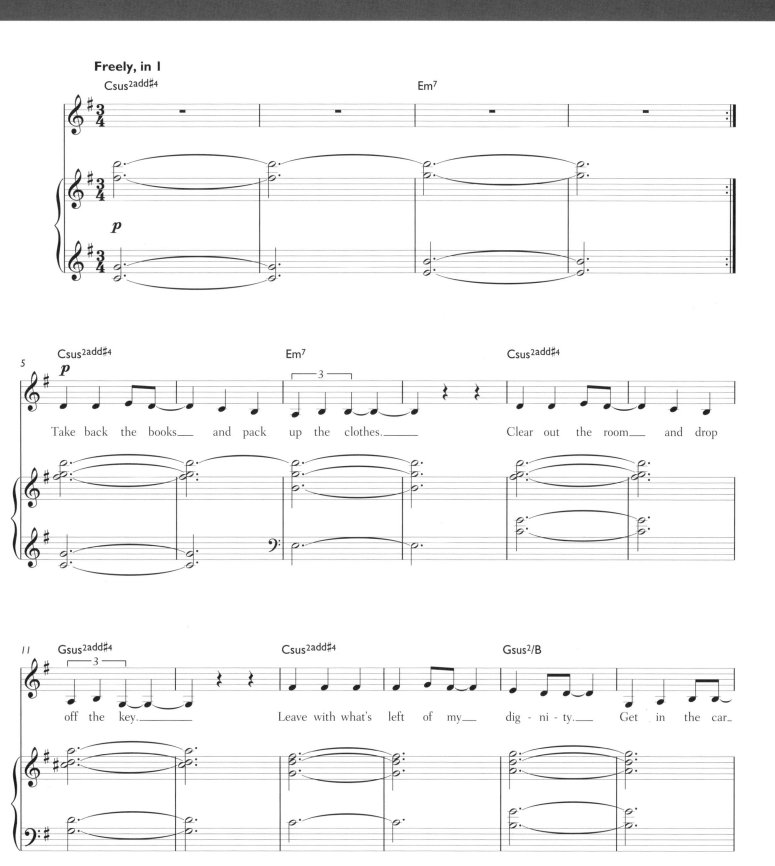

LES POISSONS

THE LITTLE MERMAID

BACKGROUND

Hans Christian Andersen's 1837 fairy tale *The Little Mermaid* is about a mermaid who gives up her voice and her life in the sea for the love of a human prince. It has been adapted for the stage, ballet, television and movies many times. The original tale has a tragic ending, with the mermaid sacrificing her life for the love of her prince and being transformed into the foam that dances forever on the waves of the sea. In the 1989 animated Disney movie this ending was changed: the mermaid Ariel lives happily ever after with Prince Eric. In the Disney tradition, a number of entertaining supporting characters were added: Scuttle the seagull, timid Flounder the fish, the villainous eels Flotsom and Jetsom, and Sebastian the Jamaican crab.

In this song, Louis, the King's French chef, prepares and cooks fish, while Sebastian, hiding in the corner, looks on appalled.

PERFORMANCE NOTES

The comedy of this song stems from the gleeful, sadistic delight that Louis takes in something so everyday as chopping up and cooking fish. In performance you can set this up from the opening line with a manic gleam in your eye when you first mention your 'love' for 'les poissons'. From the moment they hear your crazed laughter ('Hee hee hee hah hah hah') the audience should be in no doubt that they're in the company of a dangerous lunatic. A French accent is of course *de rigueur*!

The lyrics are incredibly violent: 'cut off their heads', 'hack them in two', 'slash through the skin' ... You may feel you need props and kitchen equipment to demonstrate your culinary skills like a mad TV chef. Certainly there's a lot of potential humour in a carefully choreographed routine with knives, mallets and pots slashing and bashing about in counterpoint to the brisk rhythm of the melody. Don't make this so complicated that it's distracting, though – your actions and words need to be crystal clear throughout.

The violence is offset by Louis' pride in his professionalism: his lapses into French, his mention of 'classic technique', his care in adding 'just a dab' of flour. See how delicate and precise your movement can be when you notice and pick up the 'sweet little succulent crab' around bar 61 (in the film this is Sebastian). Then end with a real flourish as you bid your victims *au revoir*.

SINGING TIPS

The key to this song is an exaggerated French accent. French uses a more nasal quality than English: to find this quality try saying the word 'hung'. Hold onto the *ng* sound. Now try singing this on one note. Keep singing and pinch your nose. You should find that the sound stops. This means that the sound is coming through the nose. You've found the right quality for this song.

Notice too that the *th* sound becomes a *z*, there are no *h* sounds, and an *i* vowel in words like 'miss' and 'this' almost becomes *ee*.

Finally, the stress in French is very often on the last syllable of the word instead of the first as in English. Really aim for the second syllable of words like 'poissons', 'inside' and 'silver'.

LES POISSONS

WORDS BY HOWARD ASHMAN
MUSIC BY ALAN MENKEN

TRACK 7

Les pois - sons, les pois - sons, how I

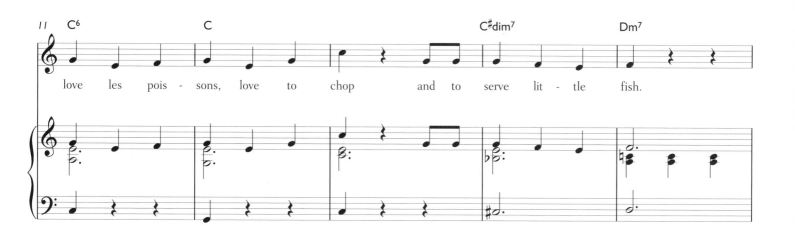

love les pois - sons, love to chop and to serve lit - tle fish.

MY DEFENCES ARE DOWN

ANNIE GET YOUR GUN

BACKGROUND

One of the most successful and frequently revived shows from the 'Golden Age' of musical theatre, the plot of *Annie Get Your Gun* (1946) revolves around the love-hate relationship between rival fairground sharpshooters Annie Oakley and Frank Butler. The show is packed with wonderful characters, brilliant jokes and an outstanding score by Irving Berlin which never stops reminding us that 'there's no business like show business'. Judy Garland was originally signed to play Annie in the 1950 MGM film version, but had to withdraw because of ill-health. Betty Hutton took over the role and the film became the top grossing movie of the year.

When hillbilly Annie Oakley beats Frank Butler – the star of Buffalo Bill's Wild West Show – in a shooting contest, she is immediately invited to join the company as Frank's assistant. While working together, Frank falls in love with straight-talking, tomboyish Annie, and in this song he prepares to propose to her.

PERFORMANCE NOTES

Frank is a man's man, the long-established star of the show, smart, handsome, used to being the centre of attention, a bit big-headed. He's always enjoyed the adulation of his female fans (with whom he's had 'lots of fun') and can't quite believe he's met someone he wants to marry.

When performing this song as a solo, address the audience as if they are your closest friends. Be entirely honest with them, admit that you've changed: I used to be like that ('a lion') but now I am like this ('a lamb'). But note who and what Frank compares himself to: a tiger, a medieval knight, Samson. What does this tell you about his own self-image?

Explore these strange new feelings as you express them through song. Allow your thoughts to develop gradually: it may be quite a surprise to find that 'I like it', quite a relief that 'there's nothing to be done'. And you can really enjoy your final paradoxical conclusion: from now on, it will be fun to be miserable! Don't be afraid to sing that out in triumph.

SINGING TIPS

Strong singing is required here, which means focused energy and effort without unwanted tension. Make sure you don't get tight through the jaw and neck. Try the following:

Gently lower the chin until it rests on your chest. Feel the stretch in the back of your neck. Now lift your chin up slowly until you're looking at the ceiling. Don't let your head go too far back: do it just so that you feel the stretch at the front of your neck. Finally, bring your chin back to the centre. When you're singing, aim for a position that doesn't stretch the neck muscles, and don't stick your chin out.

Check that you're inhaling well too. Bend slightly forward and put your hands on your back at waist-level. Breathe in. You should feel your back muscles expand. When singing with power you need plenty of activated back support, so keep working these muscles.

MY DEFENCES ARE DOWN

WORDS AND MUSIC BY IRVING BERLIN

TRACK 8

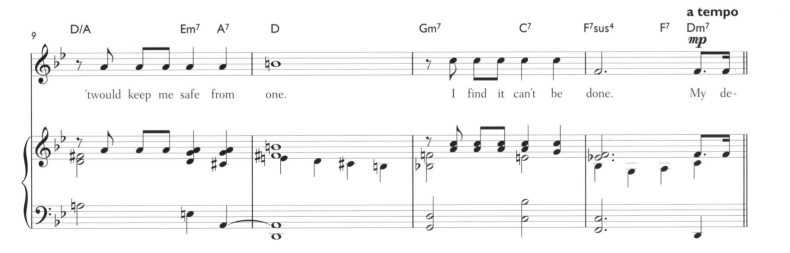

MY SHIP
LADY IN THE DARK

BACKGROUND

When it opened in 1941, *Lady in the Dark* was immediately recognised as one of the most imaginative and experimental musicals ever seen on Broadway. Dealing with the pressures of contemporary city living and the comparatively new phenomenon of psychoanalysis, the show explores the heroine's subconscious in three extended musical dream sequences which work like mini-operas within a straight play. With Gertrude Lawrence in the lead, the show became a hit and played for two extended seasons on Broadway. The 1944 movie starring Ginger Rogers made several changes to the stage show, inexplicably cutting this song, which is absolutely essential to understanding the story.

Successful fashion magazine editor Liza Elliot finds it increasingly difficult to cope with the mounting stress in both her personal and professional life. She undergoes a course of psychoanalysis in order to confront her anxieties. Only when she comes to terms with her fears, wishes and disappointments is she properly able to recall and sing this childhood song which has been haunting her dreams.

PERFORMANCE NOTES

This song comes out of nowhere. As in a movie – or a dream– we're suddenly and inexplicably presented with the mysterious image of a fabulous ship crammed with exotic jewels sailing across the sea. Where has it come from? Where is it going? Don't worry about this yet – just concentrate on recalling the details as if from a dream and sharing them with the audience. Relish the sensuous language: 'silk', 'jam and spice', 'aglow with a million pearls', 'a sapphire sky'.

The song suddenly 'cuts' – again like a film – to an image of the singer on a quayside. Now you're a character in your own dream. Time seems frozen. The lyrics are ambiguous: have you been waiting there 'for years'? Or are you talking about the years you might wait in the future?

The song reveals its meaning in the final verse. You will only be released from your endless wait when the ship arrives. But the fabulous riches it contains will be valueless if 'there's missing just one thing'. Aim to bring the song to a deeply personal conclusion: after all, only you know who or what your 'own true love' really is.

SINGING TIPS

This song has three sections or an ABA structure. The two outer parts require really legato singing. Imagine you are a cellist, drawing a bow across a string in a smooth motion; try miming this as you sing. You could also try drawing the shapes of the phrases in the air as you sing.

To ensure that the sound stays even from the bottom to the top of a phrase, practise 'sirening' on an *ng* sound, really swooping between the notes. Repeat using *oo* and feel the notes joining together. This is only for practice though! When you sing the song ensure that, even with a lovely smooth legato, each individual note is clearly centred.

In the B section try detaching the notes just a little more, using the consonants in 'can', 'wait', 'till', 'it', 'fine' etc. to give this part contrasting definition.

MY SHIP

WORDS BY IRA GERSHWIN
MUSIC BY KURT WEILL

TRACK 9

NOTICE ME, HORTON
SEUSSICAL THE MUSICAL

BACKGROUND

Seussical is a musical inspired by the popular children's books by Dr Seuss, particularly *Horton Hears a Who!* The show opened on Broadway in 2000, followed by a shorter and simpler Off-Broadway revival in 2007. A cut-down one-act 'Theatre for Young Audiences' version has also proved popular.

Kind-hearted Horton the elephant discovers a tiny planet in a speck of dust, inhabited by microscopic beings called 'Whos'. As he searches for the planet amongst hundreds of clover leaves, his neighbour Gertrude McFuzz – a shy bird with only one feather in her tail who has loved Horton from afar for years – tries unsuccessfully to get his attention and make her feelings known.

PERFORMANCE NOTES

Although the plot of *Seussical* is completely bizarre – and despite the fact that an unrequited love affair between an elephant and a bird is utterly absurd – 'Notice me, Horton' captures a particularly poignant moment in the relationship between these two characters and has to be performed with the utmost commitment and sincerity.

As the song begins, Gertrude is exhausted: crossing hills and deserts may not be so hard for an elephant, but it is for a tiny bird. Now, nervous and shy, she speaks too fast and gets tongue-tied almost as soon as she opens her mouth. Like many teenagers she hates her appearance, but clings to the hope that as her tail begins to grow Horton might notice her.

Even if you are intending to perform this song as a solo, try rehearsing with another actor as Horton. Experiment with spacing and movement: how near can you – dare you – get to him? If he's moving around in the clover do you follow him or stay still? And how are you going to physicalise these characters? Are they are an elephant and a bird? Or a big, hulking boy and a timid, bird-like girl? If you're performing the song as a duet, consider the difference in the characters' focus: Horton searching for a tiny speck of dust on the ground, Gertrude trying desperately to reach out to him across the stage. Does she hear his voice as he sings? Does he hear hers? And even though he doesn't appear to notice her, what is it that makes Gertrude decide not to give up hope?

SINGING TIPS

The opening of this song needs quick rhythmic singing with excellent diction. Try saying *mammas and pappas and granmas and granpas* a few times as quickly as you can to activate your face muscles. Don't overwork them though – see if you can say the words while very gently holding your cheeks.

The main section of the song needs a full, warm sound, which means keeping the throat open. To help you achieve this, first try speaking in a very high, 'little girl' voice. Make up a story of how unfair you think something is (maybe not being invited to a party?). As you're speaking, place a finger gently on your throat and feel how tight the muscles are. Now try imitating a deep-voiced TV newsreader. Read out an imaginary news story and put your finger on your throat again. You should now feel that the muscles are more relaxed. When you sing, try to avoid the sort of tension you felt in the 'little girl' voice.

NOTICE ME, HORTON

WORDS BY STEPHEN FLAHERTY
LYRICS BY LYNN AHRENS

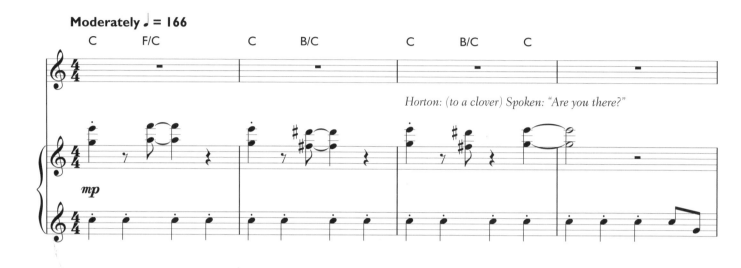

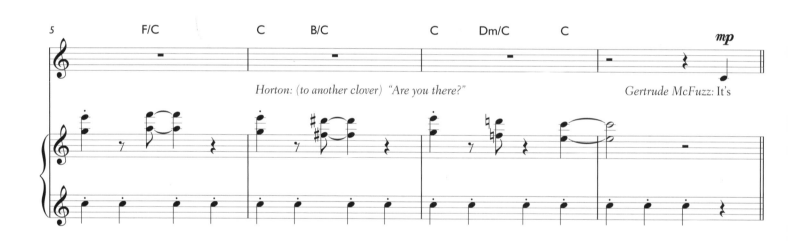

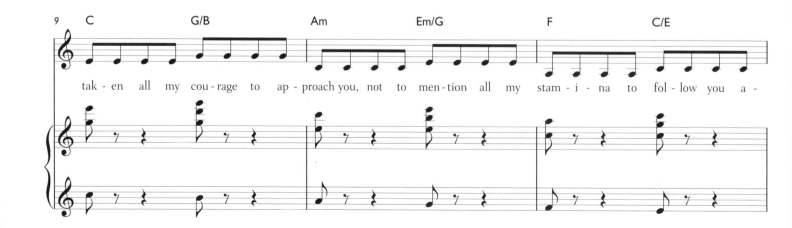

ONLY LOVE
THE SCARLET PIMPERNEL

BACKGROUND

Baroness Orczy's swashbuckling adventure novel *The Scarlet Pimpernel* was a worldwide success on its publication in 1905. The hero – who achieves superhuman feats while concealing his true identity behind a mild-mannered *alter ego* – is a precursor of superheroes such as Zorro, Superman and Batman.

Parisienne actress Marguerite St Just is married to foppish English aristocrat Percy Blakeney, little suspecting that he is in reality The Scarlet Pimpernel, a mysterious adventurer who saves victims of the French Revolution from the guillotine. When her brother is captured by the secret police, Marguerite arranges a secret meeting with the Pimpernel and – unaware she is addressing her husband – asks for his assistance.

PERFORMANCE NOTES

The original dramatic context of this song is highly complex: the clandestine meeting at night, the hero hiding in the shadows, the ever-present threat of the secret police, Marguerite desperate to save her brother yet clearly drawn to this mysterious stranger ... This tangled web of relationships may be virtually impossible to convey in a solo performance.

The lyrics, however, are completely clear and unambiguous: a woman's offer of love to a reluctant man. He initially 'turn(s) away', but their eyes meet, she senses the fact that this is a profoundly important moment in their lives ('This night begins to change who we are'), they touch hands and, elated, she encourages him to embrace the moment and find freedom and release in their relationship.

The danger is that the rather generalised lyrics may lead to a rather generalised performance. To avoid this, rehearse with another actor and explore the possibilities offered by playing the scene with different, but very specific, spatial relationships between you. How will he 'turn away'? How quickly? Does he move away from you? How many steps? How – and when exactly – do your eyes meet? How do you 'touch' – and does this happen once or several times? Use this process to heighten your awareness of the subtle nuances of the encounter between these two characters.

SINGING TIPS

Much of this song lies in what we call the middle register of the voice. However, where it builds up, and where the emotional intensity increases, you're taken into a higher register. To help the blend of the sound try the following:

Using a *brrr* sound, swoop from a low note through to a high note and back again. If you can roll your *Rs* like an Italian, do the same with a long rolled *r*. Now start on a low note on the word *you* and swoop upwards as high as you can go. At the top change the word to *we* and then swoop downwards. Make the change from *you* to *we* without a break. Keep your throat open all the time you are doing these exercises: imagine you're about to have a long drink before you sing.

ONLY LOVE

WORDS BY NAN KNIGHTON
MUSIC BY FRANK WILDHORN

OVER THE RAINBOW

THE WIZARD OF OZ

BACKGROUND

L Frank Baum's 1900 book *The Wizard of Oz* was first adapted for the stage in 1903, but most people know the story from the enormously popular 1939 movie starring Judy Garland, which is generally considered to be one of the greatest films ever made.

12-year-old farm girl Dorothy is in trouble. Her dog Toto bites a grumpy neighbour, who threatens to have him destroyed. Alone in the farmyard with only Toto for company, unsure of what the future holds, Dorothy dreams of going to 'some place where there isn't any trouble'. Soon afterwards she finds herself in the magical kingdom of Oz.

PERFORMANCE NOTES

'Over the rainbow' is a truly great song: a perfect combination of a beautiful, haunting melody and evocative, mysterious lyrics. It's also extremely well known: there's a danger that the audience will 'turn off', thinking that they've heard it all before. Your job is to make them hear every word, every thought, every idea afresh, as if for the first time. Take time to study the lyrics carefully. Note how the song moves between the grim reality of the everyday world (where life is full of clouds and troubles, where you can only 'dare' to dream) and the magical world you long for (where 'skies are blue' and dreams 'really do come true').

The song also moves between the present (although things are bad now there is a magical land elsewhere), the future ('someday' I will get there) and – almost imperceptibly – the past. Consider the ambiguous use of the word 'once' in the first verse: do you mean you heard about Oz at some unspecified earlier time you can't now recall? Or once and once only in a moment that has stayed with you forever? Dig deep into the lyrics and use these contrasts of time and space to underpin your interpretation of the song's meaning as you perform it.

The song ends with questions: if Oz is so tantalisingly close that bluebirds can easily fly there, why can't you get there? At bars 58–61 there's an opportunity for a few moments of silent reflection. At this point in the movie Dorothy looks up and sees a sunbeam piercing through the clouds. What do you want the audience to feel here? How might you achieve this?

SINGING TIPS

In this song it's important to sing with an even, full tone across the vocal registers. Try the following exercises to move easily from low to high. Starting on a low note, sing *oo*, glide up to around the third note of the scale, and then glide back down to your starting note. Gradually increase the range so that each time you're moving higher until you're gliding up and down an octave. Now do the same to an *ee* sound. Allow your voice to open up as you go higher.

Now look at the octave intervals on the word 'somewhere'. Glide upwards from the lowest note to the highest, starting on the vowel sound of 'some' (*uh*) and changing the vowel as you glide to the vowel of 'where' (*eh*). Next, sing the two notes cleanly, without gliding, on those two vowel sounds. Finally, add the consonants and sing 'somewhere'.

OVER THE RAINBOW

MUSIC BY HAROLD ARLEN
LYRICS BY E Y HARBURG

TRACK
12

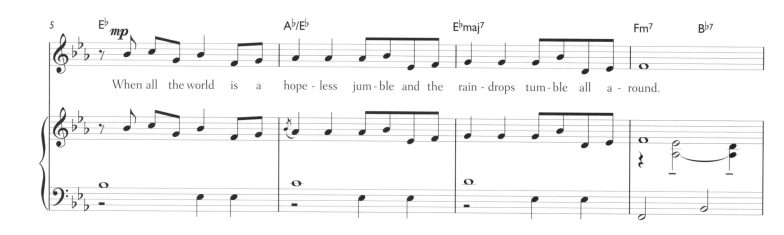

When all the world is a hope-less jum-ble and the rain-drops tum-ble all a-round.

Hea - ven o-pens a ma-gic lane.

REVIEWING THE SITUATION
OLIVER!

BACKGROUND

Lionel Bart's musical adaptation of Charles Dickens' 1838 novel *Oliver Twist* was an immediate hit when it was first performed in London 1963. It transferred to Broadway for a record-breaking run and was made into an Oscar-winning movie.

When young Oliver Twist is thrown out of the workhouse, he falls into the clutches of the villainous Fagin and his gang of pickpockets, who initially offer him friendship and a sense of belonging. But when Oliver is arrested and the police start snooping around, Fagin thinks it might be time to bring his criminal career to an end before it's too late. In this song he considers his options for the future.

PERFORMANCE NOTES

This song reveals many different aspects of Fagin's personality at bewildering speed. We're bombarded with information about his past, his current life, his dreams for the future, his opinions and his ideas – some of which contradict each other – as he tries to find a convincing reason to give up crime. The more you are prepared to share these shifts, switchbacks and changes with the audience, the richer, more complex and more entertaining your performance will be.

In the 'ad lib' sections of the song you can enjoy being absolutely shameless in presenting yourself to the audience as a misunderstood victim who needs their sympathy and friendship. See how theatrical you can be on phrases like 'Where shall I go? Somebody?' while still remaining in character. But once a possible escape plan jumps into your head, worry at it like a terrier in a frantic attempt to see where it leads you – which is of course always back to the point you started from.

Fagin is a grotesque villain. He is also Jewish. Actors in some earlier stage and filmed interpretations of *Oliver Twist* (Alec Guinness in the 1948 film, for example) endowed the character with certain physical characteristics, mannerisms and vocal affectations which many people nowadays find offensive. You need to be aware of this potential danger and exercise taste and discretion in refining the physicality and vocal delivery you use for the role.

SINGING TIPS

This song relies on excellent articulation to get the words across. Your tongue must be loose enough to work freely. Try a tongue workout before you sing. Flip it up and down, and in and out of your mouth. Put the tip of your tongue into your left cheek and then into your right one. Stick your tongue out at someone!

To get your tongue working with your lips and a nice loose jaw, try saying the following tongue twisters: *Red lorry, yellow lorry*, and *Red rooster, yellow rooster*. Sing down scales, changing note as you change from *red* to *yellow*. Try singing up a scale to *flick a flea* on each note. Come down the scale to *nineteen nifty nuns nibble nuts* or *many manic monks manage mops* to work on other consonants. Remember not to over-articulate: keep all your face muscles and your tongue free from tension. Try to let the tip of your tongue come to rest behind the back of your bottom set of teeth.

REVIEWING THE SITUATION

WORDS AND MUSIC BY LIONEL BART

TRACK 13

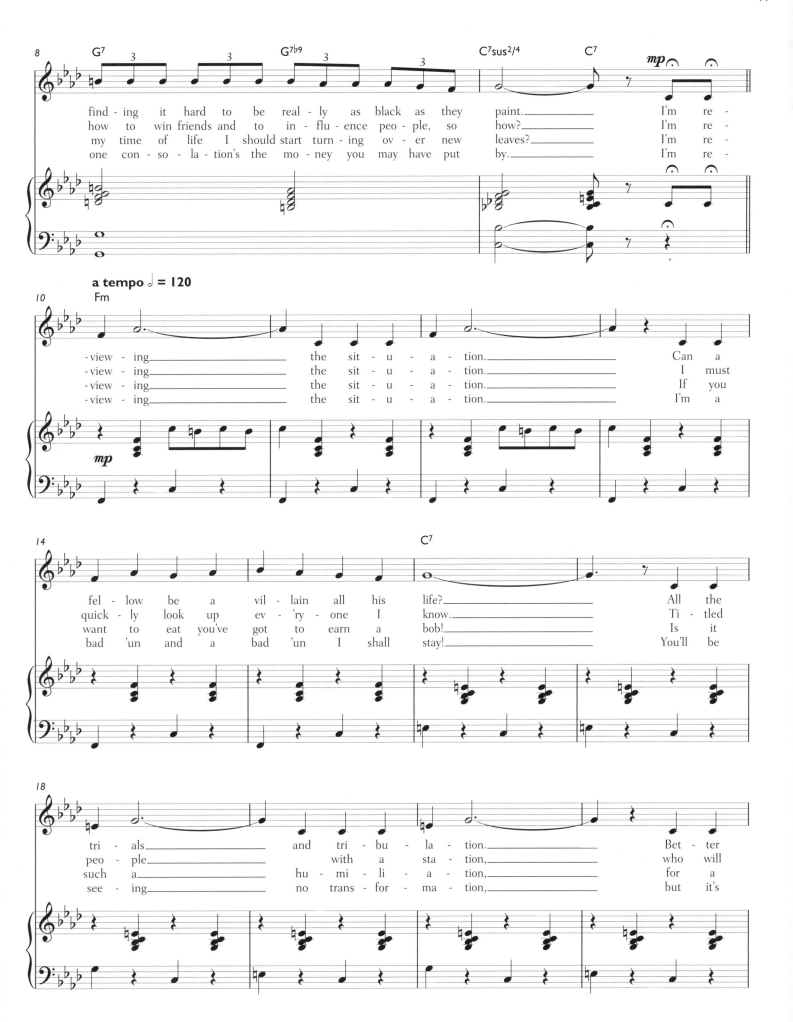

SOMETHING GOOD
THE SOUND OF MUSIC

BACKGROUND

In 1930s Austria, novice nun Maria leaves her convent to become governess to the seven children of stern widower Captain Von Trapp. She teaches them to sing, marries their father, and the family become successful concert performers before fleeing to Switzerland to escape the Nazis. Based on Maria Von Trapp's 1948 autobiography, the plot of *The Sound of Music* is one of the most famous in musical theatre.

After a long and spikey relationship with many misunderstandings and mistakes on both parts, Maria and the Captain sit in the garden one summer night and declare their love for each other in 'Something good'. The song was written especially for the movie and doesn't appear in the stage show.

PERFORMANCE NOTES

As originally scored this is a duet: Maria sings the first three verses as a solo, the repeat of the second verse ('For here you are') is split between her and the Captain, and the final verse ('Nothing comes from nothing') is sung by them together, with just a couple of solo lines each.

These are two highly sophisticated and intelligent characters, but this simple song with its straightforward lyrics is entirely appropriate for them at this point in their story. Despite the many differences between them in wealth, status and upbringing – and all their ups and downs – they finally recognise and share their innermost feelings for each other. It's fitting that this simple truth is expressed in equally simple language and melody. Indeed, it's almost as if their lives start again at this point.

Although she is not consciously intending to do so, in effect Maria 'teaches' the Captain this song just as, long ago, she once taught his children 'Do Re Mi'. But as he repeats it back to her the shared melody and lyrics take on a new and profound meaning and they realise that this is indeed the moment to which their entire lives have led them. Enjoy this experience and don't be tempted to speed up the relatively leisurely tempo – neither of you ever want this song or this feeling to end.

SINGING TIPS

This song requires a really sustained legato line. First try singing each phrase just on one vowel sound. To make sure the air flow is sufficient to get you through to the ends of phrases, try the following:

Hold your hands together in front of you, palm against palm. As you sing through a line, gradually draw your hands apart and move your arms until they're fully extended outwards away from your body. Now try reversing the movement, starting with your arms extended and gradually moving your hands together. Do all this in a flowing movement, timing the ending of each gesture with the end of each phrase.

You might also like to try singing phrases on the vowel sounds of the words, leaving out all the consonants. Feel how the shapes inside the mouth change, but make those changes as smooth as possible. Finally, when you add the consonants, don't let them break up the line too much.

SOMETHING GOOD

LYRICS AND MUSIC BY RICHARD RODGERS

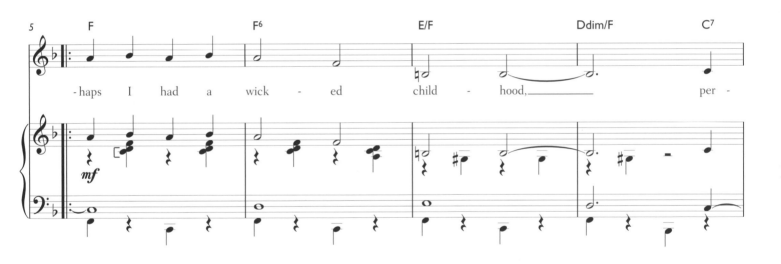

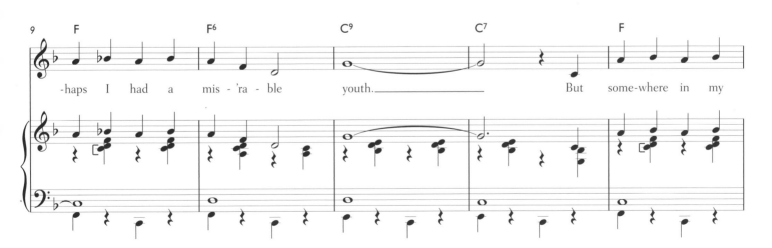

WARTS AND ALL

HONK!

BACKGROUND

Hans Christian Andersen's 1843 fairy tale *The Ugly Duckling* has been adapted many times for stage, opera and animated film. George Styles and Anthony Drew's musical version of the story – *Honk!* – was first performed in 1993 and was subsequently produced in an expanded version at the Royal National Theatre in London in 1999, winning the Olivier Award for Best Musical in 2000.

Lost and alone, Ugly the duckling wanders through the English countryside, trying to find his way back home. As he's about to give up hope forever, he meets a Bullfrog who gives him an invaluable piece of advice.

PERFORMANCE NOTES

When the 17th-century English statesman Oliver Cromwell was having his portrait painted, he reportedly asked that it show him exactly as he was, 'warts and all'. The phrase has since come to be associated with a willingness to present yourself to the world in a completely honest, straightforward, unadorned fashion. Bullfrog's appearance is so eccentric, so grotesque, that he just doesn't worry about it – and anyway, one day he'll inevitably find someone who loves him for who he is, regardless of his looks. In explaining this philosophy, he puts Ugly's self-consciousness about his own appearance into perspective and gives him a much-needed boost of confidence to continue his search.

When performing this song, remember that Bullfrog is a born vaudeville comedian, a music hall-style entertainer who just can't stop cracking corny jokes, hoofing around the stage and playing to the crowd. Really make the most of witty and surprising rhymes ('boosting / roosting', 'Tyrannosaurus Rexy / sexy'), the audience-pleasing jokes ('ass-k your mother what it's called'), and the opportunities the music offers for neat dance steps and / or comic gestures.

Work on ways of giving the audience a sense of the world 'out there', where 'just around the corner' they may find the love of their lives. You might use the repeated word 'you' in different ways to refer to audience members as well as to Ugly. But make sure you don't get slushy or romantic about the idea of falling in love. Bullfrog's outlook is not at all sentimental – in his view it's entirely realistic – and this should be reflected in your delivery.

SINGING TIPS

This song has strong rhythmic drive; feel the underlying pulse of the music. Good air flow will help sustain the energy through the singing, particularly if you are going to incorporate movement and actions into your performance. To get the abdominal muscles working, try the following: imagine that you are 'hushing' someone. As strongly and loudly as you can, say *sh*. Do this quickly a few times in succession and feel the muscles in your lower body working hard. Then blow very gently through your lips for as long as you can and feel how the muscles release automatically to take in the next breath.

You may also want to think of introducing 'speech' quality into this song to help to characterise Bullfrog. Try counting out loud from one to five in your best Shakespearean actor voice. Then find a low note in your register and repeat the numbers, still speaking but with the pitch of the note. Finally sing the numbers on that note. In your performance, experiment with moving between speaking at pitch and singing.

WARTS AND ALL

WORDS BY ANTHONY DREWE
MUSIC BY GEORGE STILES

TRACK
15

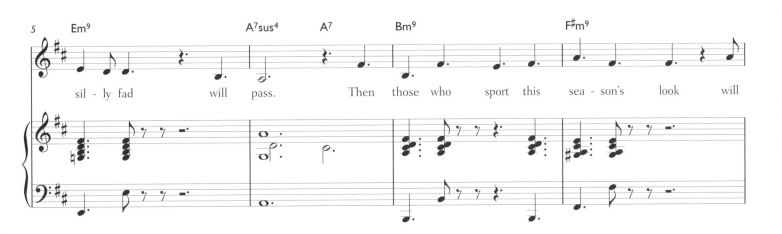

Though it may take___ some time to find 'em___ when___ you do you'll have a___ ball.___ 'Cause

out there some-where some - one's gon-na love yer___ warts and

♩. = c.190

poco più mosso ♩. = 200

all! The

sempre molto staccato

ug - li - est of crea - tures have a few re - deem - ing fea - tures so

Though it may take___ some time to find 'em when___ you do you'll have a___ ball._

___ 'Cause out there some-where some - one's gon-na love yer.___

Ugly: 'Cause out there some-where some - one's gon-na love yer.___

warts and all.

warts and all.

OTHER TITLES AVAILABLE IN THIS SERIES

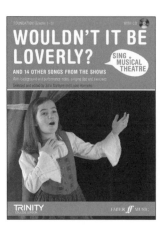

ANY DREAM WILL DO
ISBN10: 0-571-53555-0

ANY DREAM WILL DO

BE KIND TO YOUR PARENTS

A COMMON BOY

FAT SAM'S GRAND SLAM

FLASH, BANG, WALLOP!

JUST ONE PERSON

LET'S GO FLY A KITE

A LOVELY LEGGY POTION

MAYBE

MOONSHINE LULLABY

MY FAVOURITE THINGS

PART OF YOUR WORLD

ROUND-SHOULDERED MAN

THE WASPISH TANGO

WHERE IS LOVE?

WOULDN'T IT BE LOVERLY
ISBN10: 0-571-53556-9

A PLACE CALLED NEVERLAND

A SPOONFUL OF SUGAR

ALONE IN THE UNIVERSE

COLDER NOW

CURIOUSER

I WANT TO BE HAPPY

IT'S A LOVELY DAY TODAY

MR MISTOFFELEES

NO ONE KNOWS WHO I AM

SO YOU WANNA BE A BOXER

THE GIRL I MEAN TO BE

UNDER THE SEA

WE'RE OFF TO SEE THE WIZARD

WHO WILL BUY?

WOULDN'T IT BE LOVERLY?

WHISTLE DOWN THE WIND
ISBN10: 0-571-53558-5

BRUSH UP YOUR SHAKESPEARE

BUT NOT FOR ME

CLOSE EVERY DOOR

DIFFERENT

FAR FROM THE HOME I LOVE

I COULD HAVE DANCED ALL NIGHT

I WANT TO KNOW

I'M NOT THAT GIRL

MISTER SNOW

OH, THE RIO GRANDE

OOM PAH PAH

THERE MUST BE MORE

WHEN I GET MY NAME IN LIGHTS

WHEN I LOOK AT YOU

WHISTLE DOWN THE WIND

To buy Faber Music or Trinity publications or to find out about the full range of titles available
please contact your local music retailer or Faber Music sales enquiries:

Faber Music Ltd, Burnt Mill, Elizabeth Way, Harlow CM20 2HX
Tel: +44 (0) 1279 82 89 89   Fax: +44 (0) 1279 82 89 90
sales@fabermusic.com   fabermusic.com   fabermusicstore.com